Sea Turtles

BY KARA L. LAUGHLIN

The Child's World®
childsworld.com

Published by The Child's World®
1980 Lookout Drive • Mankato, MN 56003-1705
800-599-READ • www.childsworld.com

DESIGN ELEMENTS
© creatOR76/Shutterstock.com: porthole
© keren-seg/Shutterstock.com: water

PHOTO CREDITS
© danikancil/iStockphoto.com: 11; Jill Y Nightingale/
iStockphoto.com: 17; Kjeld Friis/Shutterstock.com: 6-7;
Kjersti Joergensen/Shutterstock.com: 12-13; Marjan Visser
Photography/Shutterstock.com: 18-19; Rich Carey/Shutterstock.
com: cover, 1, 8-9; Toddy101/iStockphoto.com: 14-15;
WhitcombeRD/iStockphoto.com: 5; Willyam Bradberry/
Shutterstock.com: 20-21

ISBN: 9781503816909
LCCN: 2016945609

Printed in the United States of America
PA02326

NOTE FOR PARENTS AND TEACHERS

The Child's World® helps early readers develop their
informational-reading skills by providing easy-to-read books
that fascinate them and hold their interest. Encourage new
readers by following these simple ideas:

BEFORE READING

- Page briefly through the book. Discuss the photos. What
  does the reader think he or she will learn in this book? Let
  the child ask questions.
- Look at the glossary together. Discuss the words.

READ THE BOOK

- Now read the book together, or let the child read the book
  independently.

AFTER READING

- Urge the child to think more. Ask questions such as, "What
  things are different among the animals shown in this book?"

Contents

Turtles in the Sea

What is that animal swimming by that rock? It is a sea turtle!

Sea turtles live in the world's warm seas. Sea turtles are **reptiles**. They breathe air. They must hold their breath under water.

Did you know?

There are 7 species of sea turtles.

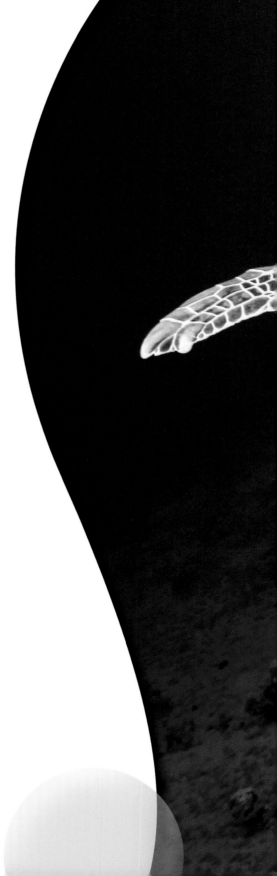

Flippers and a Shell

Sea turtles swim well. They have four **flippers**. The front flippers swim. The back flippers steer.

Sea turtles have shells. The top part is the **carapace**. The bottom is the **plastron**.

Did you know?

Sea turtles swim about 15 miles (24 kilometers) an hour.

On the Move

Sea turtles live in **feeding grounds**.
They eat sea animals or sea grass.

Did you know?

Sea turtles eat jellyfish, shrimp, and even snails.

Every year, sea turtles take a trip. They return to the place where they hatched. This can be very far away!

Baby Turtles

After the long trip, a male and female turtle **mate**. The female goes up on the beach. She scoops a nest in the sand. She lays eggs in the nest and covers them up. Then the mother turtle goes back to sea.

Did you know?

Sea turtle eggs have soft shells.

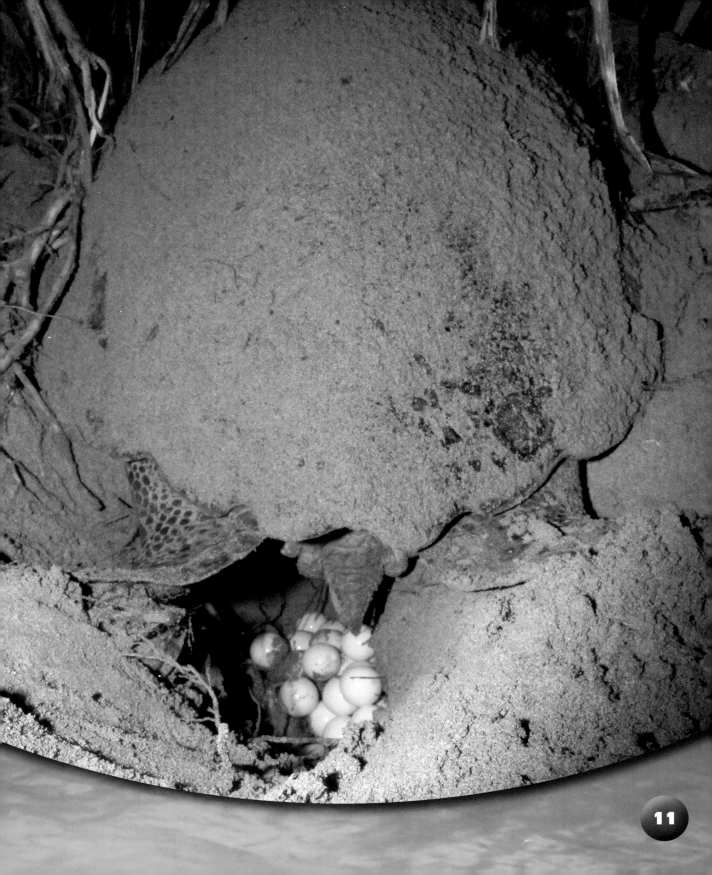

About eight weeks later, the baby turtles hatch. The **hatchlings** crawl from the nest. They scramble to the water.

Did you know?

About 100 baby turtles hatch from each nest.

The Lost Years

In the water, the hatchlings ride sea **currents**. The currents are in the deep sea. Slowly, the turtles grow.

But where do they go? How long do they stay there? The deep sea is hard to study. Scientists call this time in a sea turtle's life the **Lost Years**.

Did you know?

A sea turtle's Lost Years can last from 2 to 10 years.

Enemies

Few animals eat adult sea turtles. Their hard shells protect them. Babies are not so lucky. Many animals like to eat them.

Did you know?

Sharks, killer whales, and birds love to eat hatchlings.

Did you know?

Sea turtles are hunted for their shells, eggs, meat, and skin.

Dangers

Some sea turtles are in danger. People hunt them. Fishing gear traps them. Some people are working to protect sea turtles.

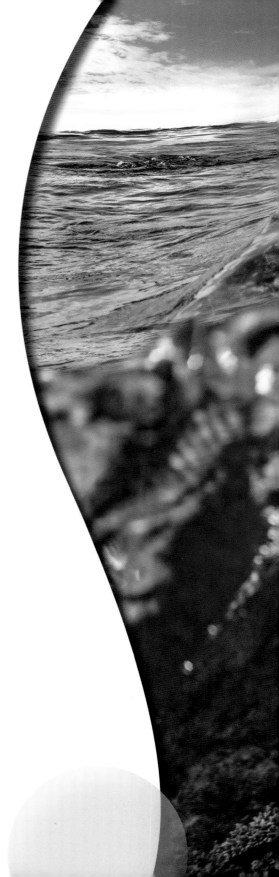

Sea turtles are the sea's world travelers. They are important animals. They are part of a healthy ocean.

Did you know?

Sea turtles can live for more than 100 years.

GLOSSARY

carapace (KAYR-uh-payss): A turtle's top shell is the carapace.

currents (KUR-rentz): Currents are parts of the ocean where the water moves in the same direction.

feeding grounds (FEED-ing GROWNDZ): Places near shore where sea turtles live and find food are called feeding grounds.

flippers (FLIP-perz): Flippers are the flat legs of some sea animals that act like paddles to help the animals swim.

hatchlings (HACH-lingz): Hatchlings are baby animals that have just hatched from their eggs.

Lost Years (LOST YEERZ): The time in a sea turtle's life that is hard for scientists to study is called the Lost Years.

mate (MAYT): When a male and female animal join together to make eggs or babies, they mate.

plastron (PLAS-trun): A turtle's underside shell is the plastron.

reptiles (REP-tylz): Reptiles are animals with bones and scaly skin. They need outside heat to keep their bodies warm.

species (SPEE-sheez): A type of a certain animal. There are 7 species of sea turtles.

TO LEARN MORE

On the Web

Visit our Web page for lots of links about sea turtles:
www.childsworld.com/links

Note to parents, teachers, and librarians:
We routinely verify our Web links to make
sure they are safe, active sites—
so encourage your readers
to check them out!

In the Library

Macheske, Felicia. *Flying Flippers: Sea Turtle.* Ann Arbor, MI.
Cherry Lake Publishing, 2016.

Meister, Cari. *Sea Turtles.* Minneapolis, MN: Jump!, 2014.

Rudenko, Dennis. *Sea Turtles.* New York, NY:
Rosen Publishing, 2016.

INDEX

About the Author

Kara L. Laughlin is an artist and writer who lives in Virginia with her husband, three kids, two guinea pigs, and a dog. She is the author of two dozen nonfiction books for kids.